Quick-and-Easy Learning Centers
Word Play

By Mary Beth Spann

SCHOLASTIC PROFESSIONAL BOOKS
New York • Toronto • London • Sydney • Auckland

Dedication

With love, to my sweet baby James.

(*"Just let Mommy finish this little bit of work and I'll be right with you, honey!"*)

M.B.S.

Acknowledgments

Heartfelt thanks to my friend and editor, Joan Novelli, for her endless patience, her incredibly sharp skills and vision, and her need to always press for the best. The high standards she sets for herself are contagious. Thanks also to Scholastic editors Terry Cooper and Helen H. Moore, two supercharged idea people who are as generous as they are bright and talented; Valerie Williams, first-grade teacher at E. M. Baker School in Great Neck, New York, for her insightful feedback and fine-tuning; and Janice Curry-Scotto, an inspired and inspiring child-centered teacher and friend whose classroom is alive with learning centers. Happily, she shared some of her learning center secrets with me so I could pass them on to you!

Copyright © 1995 by Scholastic Inc.
Design by Jeffrey Wiener Studio
Editor: Joan Novelli
Cover illustrator: Rick Brown
Interior illustrator: Jeffrey Wiener

ISBN: 0-590-53552-8

Printed in U. S. A.
12 11 10 9 8 7 6 5 4 3 2   6 7 8 9/9

Contents

From the Author

Welcome to word-play learning centers! This book has everything you need to put learning centers to work for you and your students—from tips on setting up and managing centers to complete plans for eight different activity-packed learning centers designed to foster language development in your classroom.

Each center opens with quick-and-easy how-tos for setting up an inviting center environment, and then follows with step-by-step directions for making and presenting word-play games, activities, experiments, and exercises. Tips for smooth sailing, variations, follow-up and extension activities, and literature links are sprinkled throughout. A professional bibliography offers book suggestions for learning more.

The centers in this book are designed to enhance and support your existing language arts curriculum. While students can complete many of the activities in the centers on their own, you'll find direct connections between the activities and the broader classroom picture. For example, if children will be contributing to a chart activity, it's suggested that the chart become a permanent wall display for students to use as a writing reference.

Where's the best place to start? Though you may spot seasonal links in some centers, they're presented in no particular order. Thumb through and find the ones you want to try first. As you overlay this book's offerings with your own sensibilities and experience, and add your own and your students' ideas, you can create an extra special place for learning—one that energizes your teaching and encourages a lifelong love of language in students.

—MBS

Using Centers In Your Classroom

Why use learning centers? As Michael Opitz says in *Learning Centers: Getting Them Started, Keeping Them Going* (Scholastic, 1994), "Because they're fun!" Opitz also offers a host of other valuable reasons for implementing centers: Learning centers offer an intimate learning environment—one that facilitates individual and small-group experiences, encourages cooperative learning, allows for different groupings of students, promotes every student's active participation, and more.

▷ Before you get started on setting up your centers, you'll want to think through the way learning centers will work best for you. Like any other process-based methodology, teaching with learning centers involves change, growth, and experimentation to see what works best for you and your students. It's always exciting, and this book can help make it easy!

▷ If you wonder how you'll manage a roomful of children at separate learning centers, this book will be especially helpful. As with any learning activity, the first step in successful classroom management is capturing kids' interest and keeping it going. With this in mind, the center setups and activities suggested in this book are carefully designed to appeal to children. Center settings are attractive and activities are fun-filled. But, important as that is, the real measure of whether or not a learning center is working is whether the activities hold meaning for your students.

▷ For a center and its activities to really work, students must care, or come to care, about what they are doing there. Only then will they have pride in what they learn. Only then will they want to come back for more. So even those activities that focus students on learning specific skills, such as letter recognition or spelling, must be presented in a playful way so students will gravitate to them again and again.

Putting Learning Centers to Work for Your Students

Once you understand the benefits of using learning centers in your classroom, you'll feel much more confident about giving them a go. Of course, the most important benefits belong to the students—especially young learners just starting out. For example:

- Children can work at centers independently, in pairs, or in small groups. If the activities are open-ended (and many in this book are), children can concentrate on learning together rather than competing for the "right answer."

- Learning centers wean children away from teacher direction and help them look to themselves and peers for feedback.

- Learning centers encourage opportunities for choice—choice of activities within the center and choice of which center to enter (depending on how you structure your center time and how many centers you set up).

- Learning centers provide a nontraditional approach to learning. The learner controls how to approach a task and how to spend time in the center.

- Learning centers offer choice within a context. Typically, a center has more than one offering to choose from. Allowing children some leverage in how they will structure their own time is advisable, too. (For more on including children in the learning center process, see Managing Learning Centers, page 8.)

Putting Learning Centers to Work for You

Clearly, a learning center approach can enhance students' learning experiences. But extra good news is that learning centers can help you meet your teaching needs, too—enhancing almost any teaching style because of their flexibility. Following are some choices you'll want to consider.

- You can use learning centers to enhance and extend particular whole-group lessons and activities. (In fact, many of the activities in this book are designed so that you introduce them with the whole group, then have students follow up at the centers.)

- You can use learning centers to present all or some areas of the curriculum. It's advisable to begin with a learning center that supports the curriculum area you feel strongest in, but eventually you may want to set up one for each major area of study.

- You can keep a learning center going all year (by periodically replenishing supplies and changing activities) or set it up for a limited amount of time. A yearlong center usually addresses a broad, ongoing area of study (science, math, etc.), while a short-term center usually addresses a more specific focus, such as a particular theme unit or a skill area (forest animals, money). Of course, a yearlong center may accommodate themes and skills, but sometimes it's nice to set up a center for a special focus (and it can also be refreshing to totally dismantle a center and move on to something new).

The Best Ways to Begin

As Michael Opitz says in his book *Learning Centers: Getting Them Started…Keeping Them Going* (Scholastic Professional Books, 1994), "In learning-centered classrooms especially, management is critical because students move around the room and learn to take more responsibility for their learning. Without a plan, chaos is certain." Here, then, are some tried-and-true organizational and management strategies inspired by Opitz's book.

- If you've tried learning centers before without much success, consider giving them another try. The centers and activities in this book are beginner-friendly!

- Begin simple. Begin small. Flip through the book, pick a learning center that appeals to you, and try setting up just that one. You'll notice that each center comes complete with directions for setting up an inviting area for housing the activities, such as "Spiderweb Central" and "Tinker's Toy Shop." Keep in mind that these setup ideas are suggestions only. You can modify them according to the needs and interests of your class. While most centers are a snap to put together, you may want to experiment with other decorations and designs that are right for you and your space. Sometimes your centers might be presented in a straightforward and streamlined manner, with supplies and activities collected in a decorated cardboard box. Other times you might want to create show-off centers. Both approaches (and anything in between) can work to engage your students in meaningful learning experiences.

- Put a storage system in place at the onset. Pack center supplies and activities in clearly labeled boxes complete with a list of contents—plus a list of any ancillary materials (such as resource books or children's literature) you find helpful—taped to the outside of the box. Some teachers also include a snapshot of the center so they can quickly recall what it looked like. You'll thank yourself for your efforts later (when less-organized colleagues are complaining about clutter!).

Managing Learning Centers

Once you have your learning center concept and intention in place, consider the particulars, such as: How will students visit a center? How will they rotate smoothly through several centers over the course of a day or a week? Some recommendations follow.

- Aim for a mixture of choice and expectation. Teacher-directed assignments help assure you that students experience the activities and social interactions they need, while student choices can guide you in developing new centers with students' interests in mind.

- Learn how many centers you and your class can handle comfortably. Some teachers find that rotating groups through five centers over the course of a week—one center per child per day—is a solution that works. (When children try to move through too many centers each day, they can feel hurried.) Experiment to find a combination of centers and a schedule that works for you.

- Aim to change some things some of the time. If you expect yourself to come up with a roomful of fresh new learning centers every Monday, you could be setting yourself up for frustration. If you give yourself a goal, say to reevaluate existing centers once a week, you'll be able to calmly see what you need to do to freshen some centers, eliminate others, and create new centers as the need arises.

- Keep in mind that kid-watching is one of the best learning center assessment and evaluation tools you have. So take time to watch your students as they move into a center and engage in its offerings. Ask yourself:

    - Do they know what is expected?
    - Do they seem eager to get involved?
    - Do they stay on task for a reasonable time?
    - Are they able to pick up where they left off last time?
    - What do they seem to like the best?
    - Are some tasks too difficult? Too easy?
    - What do they return to again and again?

Jot your observations in a notebook and use the information you gather to adjust your centers until they best fit your needs and those of your students.

Spiderweb Central

In this center, you'll find games and activities for helping children expand their vocabulary and use words creatively. The spiderweb theme is a reminder that, just as a busy spider works over time to spin an ever-widening, interconnected web of silk, this center's offerings will help students learn how to stretch and weave their own word knowledge and usage.

Suggestions for Setting Up

Materials

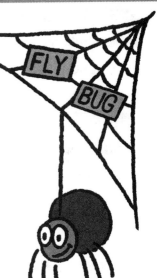

- inexpensive, reusable stretchy spiderwebs (available for about $2 at variety and party shops) or a supply of white or light-gray yarn
- heavy-duty clear packing tape or black duct tape
- medium-sized rubber band
- black construction paper spiders
- white paper or cloth tablecloth (an old sheet works well) decorated with drawn-on spiderwebs
- shoe boxes, baskets, or manila envelopes (for storing activities)
- center label reading "Welcome to Spiderweb Central"

Steps

1. Select a corner of the classroom and stretch spiderweb from ceiling to floor and then sideways to the walls; secure in place with tape. (Or measure and cut several floor-to-ceiling lengths of black yarn, including some extra length for taping purposes. Bundle the yarn lengths securely at one end with a rubber band and attach to the classroom ceiling, ceiling wire, or wall. Then fan the opposite ends of the yarn web out and attach in a circular pattern to the floor, walls, and ceiling, or flat against a bulletin board or wall. Weave another

piece of yarn in a spiral pattern through the secured yarn "spokes" to complete the webbed effect.)

2. Attach two or three paper spiders to the web.

3. Decorate shoe boxes or baskets with paper spiders labeled with activity names, and use to hold center activities.

4. Drape a table or desk with the tablecloth. Place near the web and use to display center activities and supplies.

Activity #1

Personalized Word Rings

Skills and Goals
- vocabulary
- sightword vocabulary
- spelling

Additional Materials
- markers
- crayons
- large, unruled index cards
- hole-punch
- one large metal loose-leaf binder ring per child

What to Do

1. Write each child's name on an index card. Punch a hole in one end of the card and slip the metal ring through the hole.

2. On the opposite side of the cards, have children draw self-portraits, thereby providing visual clues for the words (their names).

3. Every day, as children arrive in class, have them take turns dictating one or two additional words they wish to add to their word banks. (Stress that the words should have some special meaning to the child.)

4. At the center, have children draw pictures representing new words on their cards and then add the cards to their rings (tracing and/or copying the words if they wish).

5. Meet with each child on a regular basis (daily is ideal) and have them read the words to you. Move any word the child can't read to the back of the ring (so that all the readable words appear immediately behind the child's name card).

Variation: Personalized Word Webs

Have children choose one favorite word from their word rings. Demonstrate how to build a vocabulary of related words by placing the word in the center of a circle and drawing spokes from that circle. At the end of each spoke, have the child write and illustrate another word that relates to the word in the center. After the class has had a chance to do this exercise a number of times, place each student's pages into a booklet labeled "My Word Webs."

Activity #2

Photogenic Memory Game

Skills and Goals
- matching sight words

Additional Materials
- markers
- glue
- two photocopied photos (school photos work perfectly) or two index-card–size photos photocopied
- 3-by-5-inch unruled index cards
- drawings of each child's face

Preparation

1. Glue each photo or drawing to one index card, making sure that each student has matching photos or pictures on two cards.

2. Print students' names beneath their photos.

3. On the back of each card draw a tiny spider shape (or use spider stickers).

4. Store game cards in a spider-decorated manila envelope.

To Play

1. Shuffle prepared cards and arrange facedown.

2. Players take turns selecting two cards to turn over in an attempt to make a match.

3. Player reads the names on the turned-over cards aloud. If a match is made, the player keeps the pair of matching cards. If no match is made, the player returns the cards to their original spots.

4. When all cards have been matched up, the player with the most cards is the winner. Or, for a noncompetitive version, have each student attempt to complete all the match-ups within a prescribed time frame.

Advanced Version

Have students match cards printed with student names only. Or have students match up the names (with or without photocopied drawings) of school personnel, community landmarks, book characters, word-family sight words, spelling words, and so on.

Activity #3

Lists and More Lists

Skills and Goals
- vocabulary
- writing
- speaking

Additional Materials
- chart paper
- markers
- writing supplies

What to Do

1. Enlist students' help in making a List of Lists. Record ideas on chart paper, for example:
- words beginning with the letter S
- places you wish you could visit
- ten interesting-sounding words
- ways to have fun with friends
- things you want to be when you grow up
- things to do when planning a birthday party
- ten things you like about school
- things you would like to give away
- possible pets
- books to read

2. Post the list in the learning center.

3. Have each student choose an idea to turn into a list. Bind students' illustrated lists into a "Class Book of Lists." Or have each students create a list, write each item on a separate piece of paper, illustrate, and bind into individual books.

Extension

Have students showcase their growing vocabularies by sharing their book(s) with parents at your next open house.

Drama Treasure Chest

Children of any age love to—and indeed need to—play. In this center, each child's playful nature is the catalyst for creative language exploration. By offering students a treasure chest overflowing with dramatic props and prompts, along with activities to guide their play, you'll be setting the stage for rich oral language development.

Suggestions for Setting Up

Materials

- wooden, plastic, or cardboard "trunk" (or copy-paper box with cover)
- duct tape
- foil garland
- tablecloth (the fancier the better—try using a glue gun to attach sequins or decorate with glitter fabric paints)
- shoe boxes to hold individual activity supplies
- center label reading: "Discover Riches in the Drama Treasure Trunk"

Steps

1. Select a low-traffic corner of the classroom to set up this center.
2. Drape the decorated tablecloth over a table or desk. Place the trunk on the table (if easily accessible) or on a shelf nearby and use it to hold center activities and supplies. Provide student chairs.
3. If the trunk's lid is already attached with a hinge, check to be sure the lid cannot slam down on little fingers. (If lid is not child-safe, or if the lid is not attached, use duct tape to prop the lid open between the trunk and a wall.)
4. Drape garland around the rim of the trunk. To create an appealing backdrop, tack "rays" of garland to the wall behind the trunk.

Activity #1

Abstract Flannel Board Stories

Skills and Goals

- oral language development

Additional Materials

- flannel board
- favorite fable or fairy tale
- geometric felt shapes (purchased commercially or cut from felt scraps)

What to Do

1. Share a story aloud with children.

2. Retell the story, using felt pieces to represent story characters and setting elements. For example, when telling the story of "Little Red Riding Hood," you might use a yellow circle to represent the mother, a red circle to represent Red Riding Hood, a brown square to represent the wolf, a white circle to represent Grandma, and a brown circle to represent the hunter. You might also use a few green triangles to represent the forest. After one run-through, have students use the pieces to help you retell the story.

Tip: Try recording your story on an audiotape as you tell it to the class. Then place the recorder and tape in the center, along with the flannel board supplies.

3. Place the felt pieces and flannel board in the center for follow-up storytelling fun. In future storytelling sessions, encourage children to choose their own shapes to represent story elements.

Tip: At times, you might want to guide students' efforts, introducing criteria such as size, shape, and color.

Prop Improvisation

Skills and Goals
- vocabulary
- creative thinking skills

Additional Materials

- objects with basic shapes that could easily suggest or represent a variety of other objects (e.g., blocks, tangrams, balls, plastic hoops, sticks of various lengths, boxes, etc.)
- writing supplies

What to Do

1. Talk with students about the role improvisation plays in creativity. Explain how actors often use improvisation as a playful way to tap into their creativity and imagination.

2. Brainstorm objects that can represent a variety of other objects. For example, a yardstick may be used to represent a cane, a baseball bat, a balance beam, a telescope, a broom, a microphone, and so on.

3. Place objects listed at the center. Have students choose an object to play with. Ask them to list and illustrate other things that object could represent. Display students' lists with the corresponding objects.

4. In a subsequent sharing session, have children take turns using the objects to pantomime their ideas while the rest of the class tries to guess the pretend object.

Face-Painting Book

Pick a special occasion to encourage students to stretch their imaginations with face paints or makeup—and fine-tune their word choices as they write steps for accomplishing the look. Be sure to pretest the ingredients on each student's wrist (or as indicated) to rule out allergic reactions.

Skills and Goals

- sequencing
- written expression

Additional Materials

- construction paper
- glue
- stapler
- water-based face paints (available at party and variety stores)
- Polaroid camera and film (or drawing materials and mirror)
- book of face-painting ideas, such as *50 Nifty Ways to Paint Your Face* by Lucy Monroe (RGA Publishing Group, 1992)

What to Do

1. Show children the face-painting options in the book, or brainstorm a list of specific possibilities (such as lion-face, clock-face, daisy-face, pickle-face, monster-face, etc.).

2. Have children visit the center in pairs to make up each other's faces (according to a predetermined plan or assignment).

3. Invite children to take Polaroid photos of each other in makeup (or look in a mirror and draw pictures of their own faces).

4. Have each student glue his or her own photo to construction paper and record below the picture the "how-to" steps for the face-painting design.

5. Label each photo with the caption "Put on a _____face!" Help children fill in the blank with adjectives that appropriately describe their painted faces. Bind photos, captions, and descriptions into a class guide to face paintings.

Activity #4

Pantomime Plays

Skills and Goals

- movement
- listening

Additional Materials

- easy-to-act-out stories or plays (such as a retelling of "The Elves and the Shoemaker" to involve the whole class or *Pretend You're a Cat* by Jean Marzollo for small groups)

- tape-recording of the story or play
- tape recorder

What to Do

1. After familiarizing children with the story or play of your choice, assign children parts to act out.

2. Tell children that they will not have to speak their parts, but rather will use movements to tell the story (as the tape plays or you—or a student—retell the story).

3. Brainstorm possible movements students can employ to tell parts of the story.

4. Have children work individually or in small groups at the center to practice their parts.

5. When they are ready, invite children to perform their pantomime plays for the class.

Extension

Celebrate students' drama center learning by inviting families and other classes to a performance. With no speaking parts, the play can be pulled together quickly. On the big day, as you read the story for children to act out, consider playing some instrumental mood music in the background. Simple student-designed props can help set the scene.

Alphabet Soup Pot

What's cookin'? How about a center brimming with alphabet activities designed to foster letter recognition, letter configurations (handwriting), and sound/symbol relationships? Also on the menu are activities for identifying, comparing, contrasting, and creating alphabet graphics.

Suggestions for Setting Up

Materials

- red craft paper
- tape
- black craft paper cut to resemble large soup cauldron with drawn-on handle
- gray or yellow craft paper cut to resemble soup ladle
- unruled index cards
- assortment of large-size soup pots and ladles
- red checkered restaurant-style tablecloth (or any print or patterned covering made from paper, plastic, or cloth)
- center sign reading: "Now Serving: Souped-Up ABC's!"

Steps

1. Cover bulletin board with red craft paper.
2. Staple soup cauldron, ladle, and center sign to bulletin board.
3. Place a table near the bulletin board and drape a table or desk with the tablecloth. Arrange several student chairs around the table.
4. Place soup cauldrons and ladles on the table and use to hold and serve up center activities and supplies.

Draw-Around

Skills and Goals

- handwriting
- small motor coordination

Additional Materials

- crayons
- colored pencils
- light-colored construction paper

What to Do

1. Demonstrate tracing your hand shape on a piece of paper, drawing a series of lines around the outside and inside of the shape.

2. At the center, have children try their hand at hand-tracing, alternating colors to create patterned designs if desired.

Variation

Students can trace around letters of their names to create rainbow or patterned name tags.

Activity #2

Soup Label Letter Hunt

Skills and Goals

- letter recognition

Additional Materials

- assorted soup cans and packages with labels intact
- notepad paper cut to fit inside containers
- masking tape
- pencils

Preparation

On the bottom of each container, attach a small piece of masking tape. Label the tape with the letter, letter combination, word, or word combination you want students to locate.

To Play

1. Each student removes a blank piece of paper from inside the container and jots his or her name at the top.

2. The student then looks on the bottom of the container to discover what he or she needs to locate on the label.

3. The student looks over the label, jotting down words or sentences containing the letter(s) or word(s) requested. You could have students count and tally the number of times the letter(s) or word(s) appear on the packaging instead.

Activity #3

Bean Bounce

Skills and Goals

- letter recognition
- sound/symbol relationship

Additional Materials

- egg carton
- paper circles (trimmed to fit snugly inside egg cups)
- one bean (uncooked)
- marker

Preparation

1. On one side of each paper circle, print and underline one letter, letter combination, or word you wish students to identify. (Words selected should be culled from a meaningful source such as a story or chart that you identify ahead of time for students.)

2. On the reverse side of each circle, draw a small picture illustrating that letter, letter combination, or word.

3. Place the circles, illustration side down, into the cups.

4. Place the bean in the carton and close the lid.

To Play

1. Students take turns shaking the carton so the bean bounces from egg cup to egg cup.

2. The player opens the carton and says the sound suggested by the underlined letter, letter combination, or word, then turns the circle over to check.

3. Students set aside paper circles they select, replacing them when the game is over to set up for the next group.

Activity #4

Letter Collections

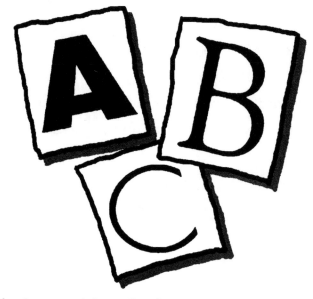

Skills and Goals

- letter identification
- contrasting/comparison

Additional Materials

- tape or stapler
- sentence strips
- discarded catalogs and magazines
- cardboard packaging saved from food, soap, toys, advertisements, etc.

What to Do

1. Invite students to each choose one or two favorite examples of alphabet graphics from the materials available, and to tape or staple their choices directly onto the soup cauldron on the bulletin board.

2. During a group meeting, have children identify and compare and contrast the attributes of letter types collected (bold and blocky, thin and curly, etc.). Help children discover that different style letters, each with a different "feel," are used for different purposes. For example, print used to advertise sweet cereals may look different than print used to advertise spaghetti sauce.

Follow-up

Have students use favorite graphic styles to create name tags for their desks and/or labels for the classroom on sentence strips.

Activity #5

Manual Alphabet Messages

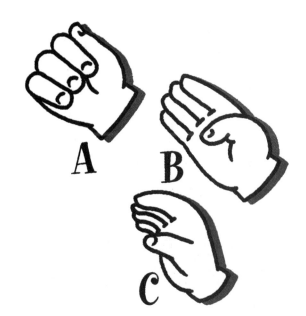

Skills and Goals
- spelling
- communicating

Additional Materials
- copy of the Manual Alphabet (reproducible page 24)
- scissors
- soup can or envelope
- glue
- paper

Preparation
Make several copies of the manual alphabet. Post one copy at the center. Cut apart others and place individual hand symbols into a soup can or envelope.

What to Do
1. Brainstorm ways people communicate. Encourage children to recognize hand symbols as one way people communicate.
2. Explain that some people who are unable to hear sounds communicate using the manual alphabet. Demonstrate by signing a simple message.
3. Have students glue letter symbols to paper to create messages to send each other or post on a class message board.

Variation
Try the same activity using cards featuring Morse code letters.

Literature Links
Chicka Chicka Boom! Boom! by Bill Martin, Jr. & John Archambault (Simon and Schuster, 1989). The irresistible adventures of alphabet letters in a coconut tree.

The Finger Alphabet by S. Harold Collins (Garlic Press, 1992). A manual alphabet activity book.

Manual Alphabet

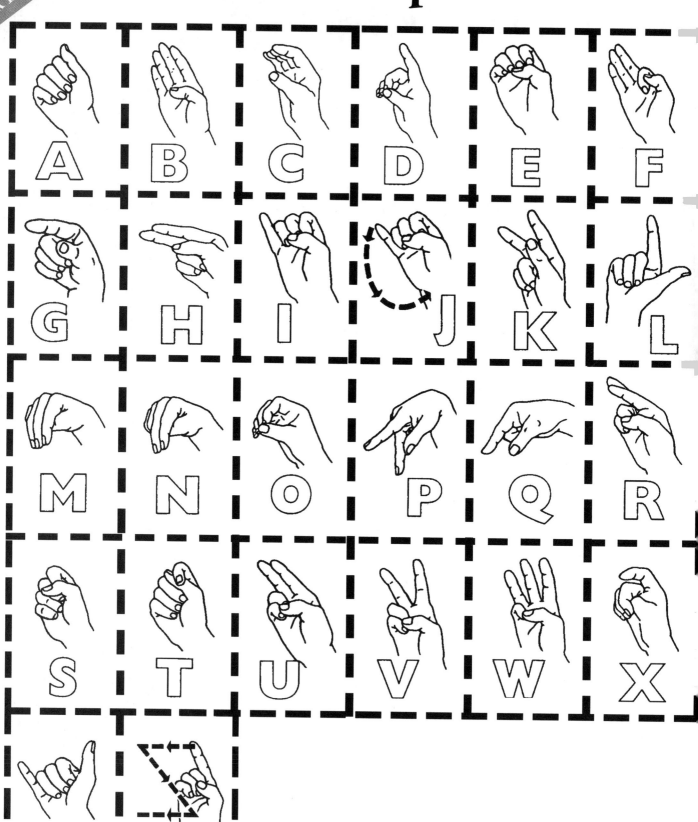

I'm All Ears Recording Studio

Listen up! This center plugs kids into listening games and activities designed for use with commercially prepared and teacher- and/or student-created audio-tapes. If you've shied away from setting up a listening/recording center in the past (or tried and flubbed), here's your chance to try again. The information here makes it easy to set up a listening center that works— it even includes a list of listening center management tips to guarantee smooth going.

Suggestions for Setting Up
Materials

- tape recorder
- headsets (optional, and not desirable for use with younger children)
- books and books on tape (commercial recordings of stories, as well as those made by students and teacher)
- blank tapes
- baskets for holding center materials
- 9-by-12-inch center sign reading: "I'm All Ears Recording Studio"

Steps

1. Reserve a table and chairs for the center. Arrange materials on table.
2. Slip center sign inside freestanding 9-by-12-inch acrylic frame and place on table.

Wordless Picture Book Wonders

Skills and Goals
- oral language development
- speaking skills
- sequencing

Additional Materials
- wordless picture books
- desk bell

What to Do

1. After sharing a series of wordless picture books (such as *The Knight and the Dragon* by Tomie de Paola and *The Bear and the Fly* by Paula Winter), place the books in the listening center and tell the children they will each have the opportunity to make a recording to accompany a wordless book selection of their choice.

2. Demonstrate equipment, including how children can ring a bell to signify page changes.

3. Be available to assist any reluctant storytellers (who may need a few practice run-throughs without the recorder).

4. Schedule class time for volunteers to share their books on tape with the class. Put them on loan at the school library.

Listen for a Reason

Skills and Goals
- reading and listening comprehension
- oral language development
- writing

What to Do

Have children listen to books and stories on tape. During each center session, have them listen for and report on one facet of the book at a time. For example, during separate sessions ask students to:

- listen for and list words they do not understand;
- listen for and list any conflicts, problems, or dilemmas encountered by the main character;
- listen for and list character descriptions;
- listen for and list descriptive words; and
- listen for and list action words.

Activity #3

Book Reviewer

Skills and Goals

- oral language development
- oral reading
- speaking skills

Additional Materials

- favorite books

What to Do

1. Ask students if they've ever seen the television show *Reading Rainbow*. Talk about the *Reading Rainbow* book reviewers. (Each show features a segment of student book reviewers who summarize favorite books and enumerate reasons other students will want to read these titles.)

2. Consider playing a segment of *Reading Rainbow* in class, paying particular attention to how the reviewers organize and present information about their books.

3. Have children write and tape book reviews of their own to share.

Variation

Videotape students' book reviews. Share with other classes and the school library. Treat parents to a viewing at open house.

Activity #4

Cliff-hangers

Skills and Goals

- reading/listening comprehension
- oral language development
- writing

Additional Materials

- new books or stories students have not read
- writing materials

What to Do

1. Begin reading (or telling) and recording the beginning of a book or story.

2. Choose an intriguing spot to stop.

3. Have students write down or illustrate their predictions for what they believe will happen next in the story. Have them share their ideas in a group setting.

4. During a follow-up listening session at the center, offer students the full book or story on tape. Have them compare the book's ending with their own.

Sentence Construction Company, Ink

Do your students think of words as powerful tools? This center is designed to help them build strong connections between words and ideas, and expand vocabulary as they become aware of word usage options, including grammar and parts of speech.

Suggestions for Setting Up

Materials

- two Hula Hoops
- marker
- tan or gray craft paper
- clear packing tape
- duct tape
- oversize plastic trucks on loan from students (or have children paint boxes to create vehicles)
- two sets of low wooden steps placed back-to-back (or a short plastic step stool)
- center sign reading: "Construction Company, Ink— We Build Sentences."

Steps

1. Create a footbridge for children to cross into the center by taping Hula Hoop "handrails" in an upright position to either side of the step stool or stairs.
2. Cover outside of hoops with craft paper cut to size. Decorate with drawn-on cobblestones.
3. Place the trucks in the center and use each one to hold a game or activity.
4. Post the center sign at the footbridge's entrance to the center.

Activity #1

Sentence Matchups

Skills and Goals

- oral language
- reading
- matching

Additional Materials

- sentence strips
- markers
- prepared language experience chart (see Preparation)

Preparation

1. Have children offer ideas related to a class theme you're working on—such as endangered animals or classroom rules. Record their ideas in full sentences on a sheet of chart paper to create a language experience chart.

2. Reread the chart with the group.

3. Copy the sentences as they appear on the chart onto individual sentence strips.

To Play

Children place the chart on the floor, examine each line, and then place a matching sentence strip directly over each line. Have children play again, this time putting sentences together without the chart as an aid. For more fun, turn sentence strips into jigsaw puzzles by cutting each strip into two or three pieces using a distinctive cutting pattern.

Tip: If students are able to look at the original whole sentences as they attempt to assemble puzzle pieces, the task is easier than if they are expected to read the fragments and piece them together without a visual reference.

Beginnings, Middles, and Endings Game

Skills and Goals

- sequencing
- sentence construction

Additional Materials

- markers
- index cards (in three colors)

Preparation

1. Select one color index card for recording sentence beginnings, one color for recording sentence middles, and one color for recording sentence endings.

2. Ask children to brainstorm a list of words naming people or things. Print each of these on a sentence-beginnings card. If the word is not a proper noun, add a modifying article or word (*A, The, Six,* etc.) printed with a capital letter to indicate the beginning of the sentence.

3. Have students brainstorm a list of action verbs. Print each of these on a sentence middle card.

4. Have students brainstorm a second list of people or things. Print each of these on a sentence ending card along with ending punctuation to indicate the end of the sentence.

To Play

Have students experiment with assembling different sensible and silly sentences by placing different beginning, middle, and ending cards together. Invite students to record and then illustrate and display their sentence constructions.

Strong Action Words

Running

Skills and Goals
- vocabulary
- parts of speech

Additional Materials
- chart pad
- self-stick notepads
- marker
- pencils

Preparation

1. Have students tell about their evening or weekend activities and record their comments in complete sentences on chart paper.

2. Help students locate and underline all the action words in the sentences.

3. Pick one verb and demonstrate how, by substituting a stronger, more specific verb, the sentence meaning is sharpened and strengthened.

What to Do

1. Have students use the self-stick notes to record stronger action words for the ones originally recorded on the chart.

2. Have students stick their new words directly over the old ones. (More than one new word may be added to each original.)

3. Take class time to read the new, stronger language.

4. Create an ongoing class thesaurus, writing action words across the top of chart paper and posting corresponding self-stick notes underneath.

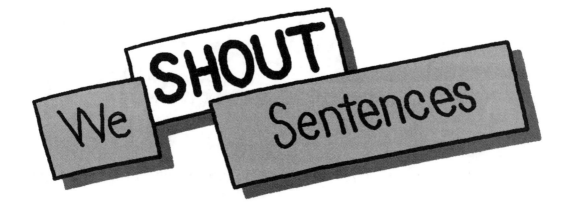

We SHOUT Sentences

Sign Maker's Shop

Some students are convinced they can't read a thing—that is until you convince them otherwise with the real-life reading activities included in this center. Using materials such as recognizable labels, containers, advertisements, logos, signs, and symbols, you can help students recognize their growing reading abilities.

Suggestions for Setting Up

Materials

- large worktable (or several desks) and chairs
- assortment of commercially prepared signs
  (purchased inexpensively or donated from a local print shop)
- duct tape
- two dowels (1 inch in diameter) or two yardsticks or metersticks
- printer's visors (check discount stores)
- plastic baskets to house supplies and activities
- center sign (cut in length to match the width of one desktop)
  reading: "Sign Maker's Shop"

Steps

1. Place one student desk and chair at the entrance to the center area; arrange remaining desks and chairs "inside."

2. Create a storefront effect by taping one dowel or stick to either side of the desk front and attaching the center sign to the top of the dowels. (During center times, students can take turns sitting at the front desk, taking orders for signs.) Use desk to store visors.

3. Post the prepared signs on a nearby bulletin board or wall space to create a print shop collage. Invite students to enrich the display with additional labels, logos, signs, and symbols they clip and save.

4. Place baskets on the table and fill with supplies and activities.

Activity #1

Labels & Logos

Skills and Goals
- sight word vocabulary
- matching

Additional Materials
- index cards
- glue
- fine-line markers
- collection of labels and logos (from food and other product packaging, and from newspaper and magazine advertisements)

Preparation

1. Mount any flimsy labels or logos on oak tag and cut apart.

2. Use the index cards to make a set of cards corresponding to the names of the labels and logos.

To Play

Have students take turns "reading" the stylized labels and logos they are familiar with and may readily recognize. Demonstrate how one or two of the same words look in ordinary printed letters. In the center, have students take turns trying to match the entire set of index cards to the actual labels and logos.

Food Label Fill-Ins

Skills and Goals
- sight-word vocabulary
- reading

Additional Materials
- chart pad
- fine-line markers
- masking tape
- collection of food labels (from food packaging and newspaper and magazine advertisements)

Preparation
1. Print the following rhyme on chart paper and on copy paper:

> **First thing this morning**
> **I opened my door**
> **And hurried on down**
> **To the grocery store.**
> **I bought some_____**
> **Some_____,**
> **and sticky jam,**
> **Then I hurried on home**
> **With the groceries in my hand.**

2. Place masking-tape loops (sticky side out) on the blank word lines in the poem.

3. Read the poem with the class. Show students how they can stick food labels directly to the tape circles to complete the rhyme. Reread the poem with labels in place.

To Play
1. Place the chart in the Sign Maker's center.

2. Have students experiment by sticking different label words to the chart.

3. Provide students with individual copies of the poem. Have them fill in the spaces in the poem with their favorite foods copied from the label.

4. Encourage students to draw pictures illustrating their rhymes.

5. Bind the collection of rhymes into a book.

Signs & Symbols Search

Skills and Goals

- sight/word vocabulary
- symbolic representation
- spelling
- shapes

Additional Materials

- writing materials
- large paper clips
- cardboard
- construction paper

Preparation

Take children on a walking tour of the school to locate and record as many signs and symbols as they can. Before starting out, provide students with cardboard "clipboards" fitted with paper clips to hold note-taking papers in place.

What to Do

1. Back in the center, have students each select a sign or symbol they recorded to turn into a realistic-looking sign.

2. Students can mount completed signs onto construction paper and add to the bulletin-board display, or "sell" at the print shop window.

Tip: You can also take photographs of signs and symbols around the school and in the community. Have students write captions for the pictures, then place photos and captions together into a magnetic photo album.

Newspaper Find and Flag

Skills and Goals

- locating information
- letter identification
- reading • spelling

Additional Materials

- highlighting markers
- fine-line markers
- newspapers and newspaper circulars
- chart paper

Preparation

1. Show students how they can use highlighting markers to locate and flag (by circling, underlining, or highlighting) information in the newspaper. Post a sample at the center.

2. Use the chart to create a series of numbered directives asking students to scan, locate, and flag particular pieces of information. For example, sample directives may read:

- Find and flag at least five words beginning with the letter *b*.
- Find and flag at least three short *u* words.
- Find and flag at least ten adjectives.
- Find the problem in one news story.

3. Have students select a piece of newspaper and record their names and the directive numbers they're responding to from the chart. To avoid confusion, you might want to have students stick to one directive per piece of newspaper.

Extension

Contact a local print shop and arrange for students to visit.

Literature Links

The Signmaker's Assistant by Tedd Arnold (Dial Books for Young Readers, 1994). A young boy finds out the hard way how powerful words on signs can really be.

I Read Signs and *I Read Symbols* by Tana Hoban (Greenwillow, 1983). Two classic books for raising children's awareness of the signs and symbols that surround them in their community.

The Tinker's Toy Shop

This center helps children discover that, like toys, words are to be enjoyed, played with, and treasured. You'll find: playful ideas for fostering basic sight-word vocabulary recognition and expansion; games for matching, rhyming, labeling, and word building (employing root words, prefixes, suffixes); as well as games for helping students identify word families and practice emerging spelling skills.

Suggestions for Setting Up

Materials

- 1/4-inch elastic bands
- ribbon
- pencil
- counting and word games
- yellow or tan craft paper
- tempera paint (assorted colors); brushes
- bulletin board or wall space
- toys such as small stuffed animals (students might like to lend their own favorites)
- recycled containers (such as empty coffee cans, shoe boxes, etc.)
- bookshelf or stacking basket unit (optional, but nice)
- center sign reading: "The Tinker's Toy Shop"

Steps

1. Cover a bulletin board or wall space with the craft paper. Sketch a shelf unit in pencil, then paint over lines with tempera paints. When dry, have students consult toy circulars and then paint on (or paste on pictures of) favorite toys on the shelves. Post center sign above display.

2. Arrange real toy shelf plus table and chairs at center.

3. Tie ribbons around toy animals' necks and attach elastic bands to the ribbons. Dangle animals from ceiling wires, or display toys on shelves or in baskets.

4. Cover containers with colorful craft paper or pages of comic strips recycled from newspapers. Place one game or activity into each container and label clearly.

Activity #1

Flip Flaps

Skills and Goals
• compound words

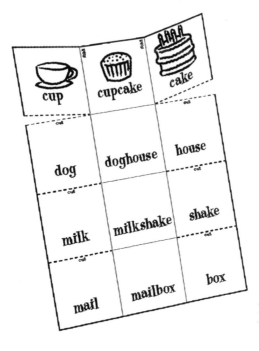

Additional Materials
• reproducible (page 42)
• scissors
• list of compound words

Preparation
1. Make a copy of the reproducible on page 42.
2. On each of the lines in the center column, print a compound word (see sample above).
3. On the left-hand flap next to each compound, print the first half of that compound word; on the right flap, print the second half of that compound word.
4. Make one copy of this master activity page for each child.
5. Show children how to cut flaps apart on the dotted lines, then fold flaps over to close them.

To Play
1. Demonstrate how the flaps open and close to reveal the hidden compound words.
2. Ask students to illustrate their pages, first by illustrating the individual words, and then by illustrating the compound words.
3. Invite children to play with their flip-flaps, opening and closing the flaps to discover new words.

Follow-up
Talk with students about how two words can come together to make a new word. Have students use blank activity pages to record and illustrate additional compound words they notice in their readings and word explorations. Children can take turns sharing their pages, opening one flap at a time and having classmates guess the compound word.

Word Dice

Skills and Goals

- prefixes
- suffixes
- root words

Additional Materials

- several square sponge shapes or plastic dice
- color press-on dots
- writing materials

Preparation

1. Use press-on dots to designate the face of some dice as prefix dice, some as suffix dice, and some as root-word dice. Print prefixes, suffixes, and root words on the dice dots. (Cull these from class charts or from books you've read together in class.)

To Play

Students place the three different types of dice into three separate cups. They then roll the dice and try to place prefixes and suffixes next to root words to make new words. Students keep a running list of their words in their writing folders and use as a writing reference.

Tip: Make several different dice at one time and rotate those you offer students so they have a fresh supply to use when playing and building their lists. Also, have a dictionary on hand for students to consult.

Literature Link

Antics! by Cathi Hepworth (G.P. Putnam's Sons, 1992). Fantastic fun for exploring root words, prefixes, and suffixes.

Word Builders

Skills and Goals

- spelling

Additional Materials

- 1-inch graph paper
- stamp pad (optional)
- letter stamps (optional)
- pencils

To Play

1. Have children play in pairs.

2. The first player stamps (or writes) a letter in any square on the graph.

3. Second player places a letter in any other square on the graph.

4. Players work together to build words. Every word spelled earns one point. A word that intersects with another word earns two points.

5. Players record words formed and keep track of their own scores. Rather than compete against each other for a high score, players can try to top themselves each time they play.

Variation

Challenge students to build words related to a particular topic or theme.

Center 7
REPRODUCIBLE

Name ______________________

fold

fold

cut

cut

cut

cut

cut

cut

An Enchanted Forest

This center's enchanted forest beckons children to celebrate childhood songs, chants, rhymes, poems, and stories as they expand language and vocabulary. This center also includes lots of ideas for interactive charts, murals, and bulletin boards.

Suggestions for Setting Up

Materials

- chart pad and chart-pad holder
- glue gun (adult use only)
- four pieces of light-brown oak tag
- two tall cardboard appliance boxes (or smaller boxes stacked and glued together to create a box tower)
- tempera paints and glitter paints; household sponge
- clear packing tape
- magic wands
- two separate star-shaped center signs reading: "Enchanted" and "Forest"

Steps

1. From the oak tag, cut two rectangular tree trunk shapes and two circular treetop shapes.

2. Use the glue gun to attach tree tops and trunks to the cardboard boxes. Use a marker to add "bark" lines and to outline branches in the treetops.

3. Sponge-paint leaves onto treetops. Let dry, then highlight with accents of glitter paint.

4. Attach center signs to treetops. Place one tree at either side of the center entrance. Place table and chairs and chart holder inside.

Activity #1

Wand Wave

Skills and Goals
- structural analysis

Additional Materials
- poem of your choice printed on chart paper
- mini-wands (staple small stars to straws or use dowels or pencils for longer-lasting wands)

To Play
Have children take turns acting as the leader for the following activities.

1. As the poem is read aloud (by you or by a student) or played on a tape, have the leader move the full-size wand beneath the charted words to underscore them.

2. Ask the leader to use the wand to locate other items of interest, such as words beginning with the same letter, rhyming words, synonyms, antonyms, punctuation, compound words, root words, silly words, sad words, scary words, color words, blends, etc.

3. To involve the audience, pass out a mini-wand to each child. As the leader works at the chart, the rest of the children can use these individual wands to underscore their own copies of the charted poem, or they can hold their wands up in the air to indicate that they hear a particular word (such as a rhyming word) or phrase as the poem is read aloud. Children can also wave the small wands in the air to keep beat with the poem's rhythm.

A Disappearing Act

Hickory, dickory, dock

The mouse ran up the ☐

Skills and Goals

- predicting
- cloze skills
- vocabulary

Additional Materials

- favorite poem printed on a piece of chart paper
- self-stick notepad

What to Do

1. Display a familiar poem on chart paper.

2. Use self-stick notes to cover up some of the key words in the poem, such as one word in a pair of rhyming words.

3. Have children guess what they think is beneath each note. Without peeking, they can each record their guesses right on the self-stick notes (signing their initials if desired).

4. When everyone has had a chance to guess, lift up the note(s) to check guesses.

Tip: Allow only four or five guesses per word, but cover enough words so that everyone has a chance to guess at least once. (You can also do this activity using individual copies of the poem. Just use liquid typewriter correction fluid to cover parts of the poem you want children to guess. Make copies of this version of the poem and invite children to record their guesses right on their papers.)

Follow-up

Repeat the activity, concealing other components of the poem (punctuation, parts of speech, etc.).

Two-Word Animal Poems

Skills and Goals
- writing
- vocabulary

Additional Materials
- sentence strips
- writing materials
- reproducible poem (see Animal Mix-up, page 47)

Preparation

1. On sentence strips print the following animal names:

- elephant
- poodle
- dinosaur
- lion
- ape
- whale
- giraffe
- tiger
- fish
- cat
- monkey
- snake

2. Cut animal names apart (whole) and place in a container. Offer each child a copy of the poem.

To Play

1. Make a class set of the poem. Have children pick one animal name at a time from the cup and then copy each name in a spot next to any one of the body parts' names they choose.

   Tip: Try this first as a class, using a chart-size copy of the poem or using an overhead so everyone can see.

2. Invite children to illustrate their poems to create graphic versions of their animals.

3. Have children read their two-word poems to each other.

4. Post poems and illustrations on a bulletin board near the center titled "Two-Word Enchanted Forest Animal Poems."

Name _____

Animal Mix-up

I am a crazy mixed-up beast of the Enchanted Forest, you see.
Just fill in all the spaces here and surely you'll agree.

Because I have a(n)

_____head,

_____hips,

_____eyes,

_____lips,

_____finger,

_____toes,

_____hair,

_____nose,

_____legs,

_____chin,

_____bottom,

_____skin.

Can you believe the shape I'm in?

Professional Bibliography

Alpha Stories: Learning the Alphabet Through Flannelboard Stories by Mary Beth Spann (First Teacher Press, 1987). A collection of 26 flannelboard stories and story patterns (one for each letter of the alphabet) with follow-up activities for reinforcing letters and sounds in a storybook setting.

Building Literacy with Interactive Charts by Kristin G. Schlosser and Vicki L. Phillips (Scholastic Professional Books, 1994). Designed to help teachers build a print-rich environment through interactive charts; tips for creating original charts, too.

Children as Storytellers by Kerry Mallan (Heinemann, 1991). Wonderful book for understanding the power of storytelling in the classroom, and the importance of helping children find their own storytelling voices. Practical classroom activities for promoting children as storytellers are sprinkled throughout.

Games for Reading by Peggy Kaye (Pantheon, 1984). A fun-filled collection of easy-to-construct learning games for practicing phonics and other reading and spelling skills that you'll want to add to your parent-lending library.

Learning Centers: Getting Them Started, Keeping Them Going by Michael F. Opitz (Scholastic Professional Books, 1994). A practical guide to incorporating learning centers into your classroom, complete with tips for classroom management, sample floor plans and schedules, ready-to-use activities, and more.

Learning Phonics and Spelling in a Whole Language Classroom by Debbie Powell and David Hornsby (Scholastic Professional Books, 1993). Classroom-tested strategies, models, and activities for integrating phonics and spelling.

Moving On in Spelling: Strategies and Activities for the Whole Language Classroom by Cheryl Lacey (Scholastic Professional Books, 1994). Everything you need to integrate spelling—from suggestions for setting up your classroom to tips for record-keeping and evaluation.

A Poem a Day by Helen H. Moore (Scholastic Professional Books, Spring 1996). More than 100 child-pleasing poems keyed to special days, holidays, and classroom themes.

Thematic Poems, Songs and Fingerplays: 45 Irresistible Rhymes and Activities to Build Literacy by Meish Goldish (Scholastic Professional Books, 1993). Need a rhyme to enrich a classroom theme? Chances are, this book's got it!